the messy in-between

a poetry collection
by kayla kim

to my fellow messy in-between travelers,

for journeying with courage and heart

to sally, lucia, natalie, kaitlyn, malia, abigail, hana, reilly, and christina,

for helping me come back home to myself

Dear readers,

As you all know, I love poetry. Writing is what brought me back to myself and to hope, what jump-started the healing and the starting over. It taught me how to find the good again, and in the same breath, how to find God. Three and a half years ago, I found myself in a dry spell of writing that lasted for months on end--I didn't and couldn't write because I felt far from myself. Three years ago, I wrote a poem called *The Messy In-Between*. That poem held the only words I could find for a long time. And with that, *The Messy In-Between* was born. I've been working on it for over two years now, and it is my whole heart on paper. It is the realest thing that I've ever written. It's the most honest thing that I've ever written. I've been gathering the courage to share my whole story all this time, and it is here now.

I wanted *The Messy In-Between* to capture the brokenness and beauty of life in a real and nuanced way. This collection required me to sit with myself, my words, and the world for as long as it took for me to create something honest. For the first time in my life I wasn't in a rush, and for the first time in my life it didn't have to be perfect. And I discovered that there was abundant beauty and goodness to be found in the process of becoming.

In seasons of hopelessness and loss, all I could do was write love letters--to the heartbreak, to the questions, to the beauty, to myself, and to a big, broken world. This collection split me wide open and healed me all at once.

Hear me when I say that this book has been a labor of love from beginning to end. My heart knows pain and grief well, and it is with deep hope and assurance that I speak the truths that I have come to know for myself throughout the years. I hope and pray that you will see yourself and your story in these pages. I hope and pray that you will find the strength to remain soft and open to the possibility of love, even when it has hurt before. I hope and pray that you will continue to let the healing come, and that you will dare to let yourself be human and beloved all the while.

So here it is--my heart on the pages, my third and newest collection, *The Messy In-Between*, in all of its messiness and beauty. You are loved, you are loved, you are loved.

With gratitude,

Kayla Kim

to the messy in-between,

you transform brokenness, pain, and everything that i have ever lost into the most beautiful love story--it brings me to my knees every time

the messy
in-between

a poetry collection
by kayla kim

the messy in-between

they never told me
just how hard the
healing would be
there are no quick
fixes around here
no right or wrong
just one foot in front of the other
each and every day

the going is slow and
the road is one less travelled
this in-between is messy
and hard to love
i am not always sure if it is worth it
but i press on
one foot in front of the other
each and every day

the sun has risen and set
a dozen times, and i am still
so far from where i want to be
i wish i wasn't afraid
but i am terrified
i wish every time
i took one step forward
i didn't take two steps back

the sun has risen and set
a dozen more times and
in the darkness come the questions
questions like
how much longer until i arrive
how hard will it get before it gets better
and the one that haunts me the most
how much more hurt until the healing

my feet carry me though they are tired
through the painful and messy and hard
this journey is painful and messy and hard
but also infinitely and unexpectedly
sweet, beautiful, honest
real and right
my feet stumble in the darkness and
find music, and i dance until the sun rises

my feet have carried me to an open field
and the stars have never looked lovelier
than they do tonight
and i have come a long way
what a difference a little time
and a little faith can make
one foot in front of the other
each and every day

-*the messy in-between*

the messy in-between

there are no words for
this kind of emptiness
i would know
i have been searching
for them for days
and they have still not come

six months have passed
and the page is still blank
and i am still crying
struggling to find the
right string of words
to cut through the hurt

a year has come and gone and
i worry that the poetry inside of me has
withered up. packed its bags. and left.
so i do what i have done before
get down on my knees
and scramble for words in the darkness

at first, they come slowly
like an unfamiliar whisper
then faster, like a song
you've known your entire life
the kind you scream at the
top of your lungs with your
best friends and windows down

so this is my best friend
window down kind of song
my love letter to a beautiful
and broken world
my right string of words
to cut through the hurt

and it is like me
imperfect and human
broken and flawed
in a thousand ways
but still worth sharing
still worth loving

and so i write
because my story matters
i matter
and you do too
i finally found the words
and they are

you are loved and
you are not alone
the sun will rise tomorrow
and nothing lasts forever
even the hurt
the healing will come and
what's lost can always be found

the messy in-between

you can't stop crying
repeating over and over
this isn't real
this isn't real
and i can't stop thinking
about how we need
to tell the truth about
how hard it is sometimes
this life can be
so hard sometimes

it's days like these
you can't stop crying
in parking lots and bathrooms
it's all the same
and you can't stop wondering
if the sadness will ever leave
if it really does get better
it's times like these
i need you to know that it will

it's nights like these
you can't stop crying
the hours pass but
you haven't slept in days
and i can't stop writing
writing poems that say
you are loved and
you are not alone
you never were
you never will be

it's weeks like these
where all you feel like
you know how to be is
broken and afraid and alone
that you can't stop believing
believing in the healing
the good that is coming
if you hold on
just a little while longer

the messy in-between

i.

these days
i am convinced
that i am entirely alone
in this world
i lay awake at night
hands clasped together
hoping
praying
that when the sun rises tomorrow
i will have the strength
to rise with it
in the darkness come
the questions
questions like
where does happiness go
when it leaves a person's body
does it enter the air the same way
it exits my bloodstream
in my absence
does it disappear
or does it multiply
does it want to be found
or is it lost forever

ii.

these days
i am convinced
that the weight of the world
is mine to carry
i lay awake at night
hands clasped together
hoping
praying
that tomorrow will be the day
that i will be enough for them
will i ever be enough for them
with the exhaustion come
the questions
questions like
if not now, then when
if not me, then who
how dare i rest when
there is so much to do
how dare i rest when
my worth lies in
what i can give
and the weight of the world
is on these shoulders

the messy in-between

iii.

these days
i am convinced
that love
is conditional
i lay awake at night
hands clasped together
hoping
praying
that this time around
you'll stay
what do i have to do
for you to stay
with the fear come
the questions
questions like
will love always hurt like this
will it always
drain me like this
will i always have to
fight for it to be mine
or does unconditional love
exist out there
maybe even for me

iv.

these days
i am convinced
that all that i am
is not enough
i lay awake at night
hands clasped together
hoping
praying
that you will remind me
of who i am again
but you do not get
the final say
with the loss come
the questions
questions like
who am i when
you are not here
and why did you
have to leave again
how can i go on when
you don't love me anymore
what if i never get better
and it always hurts

the messy in-between

to this day
you are what i am
most afraid of
in this world

i came to you whole
curious, full of life
and left broken
tender and exhausted

to this day
i am still reeling
from the aftermath
of you

the messy in-between

in the aftermath of
a love that breaks
far more than it mends
you will not always know

what is real
and what is not
you will stumble in the dark
unable to find the light

the guilt will threaten
to swallow you whole
your own story, too heavy
to carry all on your own

you are crumpling under
the weight of what
has happened to you
you cannot tell a single soul

and when you have nothing left
but your own heart
shattered in a million and
one pieces on the floor

you will begin to know
heartbreak intimately
like a close friend
like a bitter enemy

-aftermath

the messy in-between

after you
i had to learn
how to fall again
how to freefall
back in love with life
the sky and myself

but i swear falling
never felt so good

the messy in-between

abuse is abuse is abuse
and your love is not
really love at all

the messy in-between

my friends will call later
and i will clench my teeth
swallow the lump in my throat
my voice will crack
but refuse to break
i will not cry
not here
not now
the tears will come later
they will stay for three months

-the beginning

the messy in-between

when you see her
tell her that i am sorry
tell her that she's not alone and
that she will make it through
tell her that the sadness
won't last forever and
that when it has left
found another home
i will make her proud

tell her i'm sorry for forgetting
forgetting what it feels like
to be broken and afraid and alone
i used to feel so broken
and afraid and alone
i've been running ever since
i'm sorry for forgetting
what i swore to myself
i never would

tell her i'm sorry for leaving
leaving when i found my way out
for not bringing her with me
i convince myself
it's easier this way
that i have come too far
to turn back now
i'm sorry for leaving
and never looking back

tell her that it will be her
that will teach me how to cry
how to pray, how to sit
with others that feel alone
tell her that she is filled with poetry
the words will help me remember
the stanzas will help her find her way
tell her that i will make her proud
when she does

-to my 18-year-old self

the messy in-between

tonight, the voices
in my head are deafening
every single lie you taught me
memorized on my lips
they convince me
that i am alone and
remind me i am afraid
i am too broken
to be loved today

and for so long
i let the lies be as loud
as they wanted to be
let fear call the shots
but no more
my life is far too messy
and far too precious
to listen to these lies
for a single second longer

i am taking back
what has always been mine
reclaiming my life
coming back home
choosing to speak softly
even when i cannot drown out
the sound of you telling me
i am not good enough
i refuse to scream

i will declare it from the rooftops
whisper it to strangers in passing
repeat it in the mirror every day
until it becomes something
that i finally believe
today, i am enough
today, i am enough
until it silences every voice in my head
every single lie you taught me

the messy in-between

they say you're gone
and that you're not coming back
and for the first time
in a long time
i feel like i can
breathe again
feel like i have
the permission
to live again
to find the good
yet again

-*the day you left*

the messy in-between

it's been the hardest
two years of my life
but the healing is here
it has found me
where have you been
dear friend, i have
been waiting for you
all this time

is this what freedom looks like
is this what hope feels like
is this what poetry sounds like
is this what i have been
looking for all along
are you what i have been
looking for all this time

there is beauty
in this mess
in the truth that
good things come
to those that wait
just you wait
soon it will be finished
after all this time

the messy in-between

i am beginning
to forget the ways
we fell apart
and i am sorry
for the way we turned out
i let the anger and hurt
live inside of me
it is gone now
i am ready to
begin again

-begin again

the messy in-between

i used to think love
looked a lot like them
but not anymore

loving them felt
like suffocating
tell me how i'm
supposed to leave
when i can't even breathe
i beg the oxygen
in my chest to stay for
just a little while longer

at its best
toxic love feels
like gasping for air
that never comes

i used to think love
looked a lot like them
but not anymore

i am starting to think
that love might
look a little like you

loving you feels
like hoping
hoping that you won't leave
tell me you'll stay with me for
just a little while longer
tell me that i don't need
to be afraid anymore
that fear has no place anymore

at your worst
you are still
the freshest air
i have ever tasted

loving you feels
like breathing again
like living again
like coming back home
your love is freedom and
your friendship, redemption
it is just the
sweetest thing to me

loving them taught me
that love was
conditional
that it was supposed to hurt
loving you teaches me
that love is
choosing someone
each and every day
because they're worth the fight
opening yourself up
to both the hurt and the healing
and not flinching
or looking away
love is both extravagant and subtle
ordinary and radical
consistent through and through
love is showing up
coming as you are
doing it scared

most of all
i think that love
is trying our hardest
to make it all worth it
the risk and the pain

and after everything
has been said and done
i think that love
looks a little like you

the messy in-between

i welcome you at the door
with a smile but
my hands are shaking
it's been a long time
since i last let someone in
these walls don't know guests and
these floors don't know visitors
this heart doesn't know
what love is quite yet

you grace the threshold
as if it was yours
and i hold my breath
if this is my house of cards
you are a mighty gust of wind
and i am wondering why
i decided to let you in
this heart doesn't know
what love is quite yet

you find yourself
in the living room and
stop to kick up your feet
i am struck by the way
you don't seem to mind
the mess, you say that
the chaos suits me
this heart doesn't know
what love is quite yet

you walk down the hall
tracing every crack in the wall
you throw open every
closet door to find the
skeletons that hide there

i am struck by the way
you don't flinch or look away
this heart doesn't know
what love is quite yet

you ask if that's all i've got
surely, there must be more
i laugh and say, *just you wait*
in the attic there are
cobwebs and ghosts
that have never seen the light
but you've never been afraid of the dark
this heart doesn't know
what love is quite yet

you turn to me
and ask if you can stay for awhile
and just like that
you have turned an
abandoned building of hurt
into an open house of hope
and what a beautiful thing that is
this heart has never known
love like this until you

you are breaking down
the walls of this paper house
and dancing in the open space
stomping on the foundations
like it's your very own place
i am being made new from
the inside out, and with you
this heart is learning
how to let love in
one more time

the messy in-between

i know we are practicing
our *thank you*s and
our *sorry*s don't mean
what they used to
but you have to know that
i am sorry

i am sorry for the ways
that i want to love you
but will fall so short
and on my face
a million times
and then some
i am sorry for the ways
i have hurt you
and will hurt you
for the times i call too much
or not at all
for the times
i can't find the right words
and can't seem to get it right
for the times
i miss a couple texts
here and there
all your birthdays
year after year

forget what matters
that you matter
say things i don't mean
and do mean things i can't say
out loud, all i can say is that
i am sorry

so now
when *sorry* is the only word
memorized on my tongue
and the shame threatens
to swallow me whole
i practice the art of apologizing
believing in this radical thing
called grace
the radical idea
that you can and will
are capable of
loving me through this mess
that though the storms will come
we are going to be just fine
i practice believing that
with every *sorry*
there is a *thank you*
and that healthy love
can begin again with you

-*sorry and thank you*

the messy in-between

i tell you there's
no need to apologize
for coming as you are
you ask me *why*
and i can't help but weep
sweet friend, dear friend
aren't you tired of
apologizing for
the ways it still hurts
it's okay that it still hurts
i will show up every day
until you believe that
i am not here to hurt you
i am not here to hurt you
these days
you look at me like i might
disappear any second now
i search for the right words
and find your arms
i am not going anywhere
i am not going anywhere
i am here to stay

these days
your eyes and shoulders
carry the weight
of the world
they know heartbreak
feel the ache of
the in-between
sweet friend, dear friend
it's been another hard
and unpredictable season
hasn't it
but in the loneliest and
darkest times, the times
you thought you'd feel
most alone in this world
you must know
you were never alone
you were never alone
i will show up every day
until you believe that
you are always loved
you are always loved

and so now
when the word
sorry rises up
like a song you've known
your entire life
we practice *thank you*
like a new muscle
like a new language
we say with shaking hands
and trembling voices
thank you for not hurting
thank you for not leaving
thank you for trying
thank you for staying
thank you for being here
thank you for loving me
and so it begins
the hurting and the healing
a bittersweet medley
the most beautiful of duets
you and me
thank you and always

-thank you and always

the messy in-between

they told me that they loved me
but always found a reason to leave
so i learned to let go of people
that looked like you
like hope and like promise
if this is love
i don't want any part of it
if this is love
why does it hurt like this
this heart has been hurt
so many times
it cries, begs for you
to look away
for i am not worthy
i am running to
my hiding place
slamming the door
and swallowing the key
no one can enter
or leave
do not follow
do not look
and do not touch
you do not understand
this heart doesn't know
what love is quite yet
it knows conditional
and it knows fear
but it doesn't know you
for a moment i let myself
hope that you'll stay

hope that you won't leave me
like the others
but before i can find the right words
that are stuck in my throat
i see that you are already running
a million miles an hour
towards me
towards the door
you wait outside all night long
i sit on the other side
all night long
wondering where you have come from
please don't go
what did i do to deserve love like this
please keep loving like this
when the morning comes
the hope finds me too
as you unlock the door
inside there is a new beginning
you run to hold me
in your arms
i know compassion
in your arms
i begin to come home
in your arms
you tell me that i am loved
and that you will
never leave me
and just like that
this heart finally
knows what love is

-*here to stay*

the messy in-between

people do love you
even when it doesn't seem like it
even when you feel
the same as you did
all those years ago
scared and little
and alone

your heart will still know
kind, steady, and vast love
you will rest well
and laugh easy once more
and i hope you never
go to sleep thinking otherwise

-you are loved you are loved you are loved

the messy in-between

on my worst days
i am convinced that
perfection is what makes me
worthy of their love
it's days like these
i think maybe, just maybe
i am a little too broken
for them today
i cannot be everything
they want me to be
i cannot bring myself
to rise, to look
them in the eyes
the shame is too crushing
my own weight, too heavy
to lift my face and tell them
that i haven't been okay
for a long time now
for a long time now
i have been searching
for a soft place to land
a place to call my own
my entire life has been
one grand performance
a different city every night
the same spotlight and
unforgiving audience

every night is the same
holding my breath for applause
that never comes
so today, i dare myself
to walk away
from the stage and the lights
from everything i've ever known
with the bold hope that
there is more to this life
than this performance
the hustling and the striving
i walk away with the courage
that the love i have always wanted
has always been right here
right under
my feet and my fears
for a moment i allow myself
to just dance, i dance
in the streets and on the tables
for i have decided that
i cannot be contained
by your stages
today, i cannot and
will not fight to earn
what has always been mine
today, i take my final bow
today, i am free

-*the show will not go on*

the messy in-between

my whole life
has been one big performance
earning, pushing, and striving
to prove my own worth
convincing myself that
being perfect was the
only way to earn love
chanting it like a curse
more perfect, more love
more perfect, more love
over and over again until
it became everything to me

nobody ever told me
that it was all right here
my worth
in the silence
and stillness
in who i am
not in what i do
not in the accomplishments
or awards
not in the hustle but in the heart
nobody ever told me that
i am worthy just because

because for as long
as i can remember
i've had it all wrong
placing my worth in things and in people
believing that i was only as
beautiful, special, and capable
as they said i was
if praise was love, i wanted it
so when they said jump
i asked how high and
when they said more, i did
but it was never enough

so today, i choose to believe
that i am enough
no matter what they say
and when they ask me why
i will tell them that
i am imperfect and broken
human and flawed
but still worthy of love
this time i will whisper it
to myself like a lullaby
broken and loved over and over again
until it becomes who i am

the messy in-between

every night, i tuck
myself into bed and
learn how to fall a little
more in love with the body
that lays with me

because for my entire life
i have broken the only thing
that was ever mine
sacrificed it on the altar
of beauty and success

no more and
not a second longer
never again will i force
this body to be what
it was never meant to be

i am reclaiming these legs
they carry me back home
i am looking down at this body
asking how so much light and goodness
can be contained inside flesh and bones

for even when i was not
entirely convinced i mattered
this heart just kept on beating
every molecule of my being
insisted on being

you can't possibly tell me
that i do not belong here
when i have been given a body
that has fought to keep me here
i will learn how to love it now

the messy in-between

it is 2am again
and my eyelids can't hold
the demands of the day
my shoulders can't carry
the weight of the world anymore
these bones are tired
this soul is dry
living on shadows of monday
and all i know is
i don't know how
i got this far from myself
tell me how to find my way back
i am not sure where
i learned to mistake
more for better
perfect for good
rest for selfishness
what i do for all that i am
tell me where i can unlearn these lies
tell me what to do
when their plans for me
are more than i can give

the messy in-between

and i am doing it
oh, how i am living
but then you tell me
your heart has been aching
these days and
i feel my heart breaking
for pain that is not my own
and this is how
you lose me and
find me all at once

-this will be the end of me

the messy in-between

and just when i had finally
gotten you out of my bloodstream
you text me at 2am saying
i miss you, can we try this again
and i'm surprised at
how little you need to say
for me to almost take you back
right there in that moment
i would
but then i remember the first time
about how missing you
turned into ruining me
and ever since then
i promised myself
i would never give anyone
the power to destroy me
so here i am
walking away
from you again

the messy in-between

i have always been terrified
that people would love me less
if they knew the real me
if the worst thing happened tomorrow
who would rush to my side
if i let myself be seen
who would stay
if i let myself be imperfect
who would love me all the same
a part of me still trembles
at the thought that
in a world of 7.8 billion people
i am still completely
and utterly
alone

-*what are you most afraid of*

the messy in-between

i come to the page again
unsure of what will come
i have been calling
begging for poetry
that has not come in months
it's been months since
the words have danced
with the silence

four months have passed
and i am convinced
that my hands have
misplaced the lines
my eyes have lost sight
of where they belong
my mouth has forgotten
how they taste

five months have passed
and i am homesick
for who i used to be
will this body
ever be a vessel
for imperfect art again
tell me who i am when
i am this far from myself

the messy in-between

i have not come
and laid my heart
on these pages for awhile
but my heart is too heavy
for me to carry all on my own

the messy in-between

i want my whole life
to be poetry
my existence
living, breathing art
i come to the page
with my heart on my sleeve
telling stories that are
only mine to tell
speaking truth the
only way i know how

the words pulse
through my veins
as if they are
what keep me alive
they may very well be
my tears saturate the ground
my words hang
suspended in the air
the earth opens itself up
to reveal a garden

the magic is inside of me
let my body be the vessel
let my poetry be the music
i need them to know
that they are not alone
i need you to know
that you're not alone
let my whole life remind you
that you are not alone
let my whole life be poetry

the messy in-between

find people that
bring out the poetry
inside of you

-and don't let them go

the messy in-between

there is nothing
in the universe
like art that comes from
deep within yourself

nothing quite like our stories
broken, messy, and human
beautiful, intentional, and ours

the messy in-between

it's nights like these
i can't sleep
dreaming about
how far i've come
and how far i'll go

-hope

the messy in-between

let love be the single thing
that grows inside of us
until it cannot be contained
a single second longer
let us give out of the abundance

the messy in-between

i am hurting
i am growing
i am hurting
i am growing

the messy in-between

the heart always wants
what it cannot have
and maybe that is why
my heart aches for homes
i left for others

the messy in-between

my heart shattered
in a million and one
pieces yesterday and
i am no longer sure
what is real anymore
all i know is that the
hurt has found its way
back into my life again
and the celebration
has been taken from me
one more time
and another good thing
has refused to stay

i wonder if it will
always be this hard
if i will always
be this broken
if the healing will
always feel this far
where is the finish line
the light at the
end of the tunnel
every time i crawl
an inch closer
they move the finish line
a million miles farther

tell me where to
find the strength
to keep going in a
race i can never win

where do i find
the courage to
strive for a prize
that is always just a
little out of my reach
i thought the healing
would have found me
by now, but i am
still. so. broken.

i used to hope
and i used to dream
but look where
that has gotten me
this heart is too weary
to find the good today
to keep showing up
only to be let down again
the healing has spit me
out whole, for it does
not want me anymore
it does not know
how to stay the way
i need it to anymore

yesterday, i mourned
the loss of an old friend
redemption, for i am
the same as i once was
i used to be so convinced
that i was healing
but i am still so far

from who i thought
i was becoming
am i really growing if
after all this time i am
still. so. broken.

i was so sure
that life would
be easier by now
that i wouldn't
have to hurt anymore
i wanted the healing
so badly that i almost
convinced myself i had it
i really thought i had it
but those plans
have been shattered
clay into rubble
rubble into dust

it is here in the dust
that the hope finds its way
back into my life
once again, for though
we may not arrive
we can become
and though we are broken
we are loved, and the hope
can't help but find me again
like a stubborn flower
like a beautiful thing
out of dust

-beautiful things out of dust

*inspired by gungor

the messy in-between

and while
my heart has shattered
a thousand times
only to heal
and break again
i consider it all gain
knowing that all
that is beautiful and good
in this life is not
without its own pain

the messy in-between

today
you spoke over me
the same promise
you have been
whispering to me since
the beginning of time
and it sounded like
a song i've known
my entire life
with different chords
the symphony is enough
to bring me to my knees
and carry me back home
today, i am coming back home

in my hardest battles
and harshest storms
you fought for me
armed yourself with
a bigger plan and
declared your victory
over the darkness
you whisper to me
just you wait
for there is so much more
i am not finished yet

though the battle was long
and the rain kept on
pouring down
you remained faithful
in fighting a fight
that was too big for me
though i do not know your plans
the battles and hurts
that await me
i cling to your promise
listen for the soft voice
in the back of the room
whispering to me
just you wait
for there is so much more
i am not finished yet

in the deepest valleys
the shadow of death
you held me and whispered
there is so much more
over and over again
until morning came
surely, there will be
more of this hurt
but i am not ready
to give up just yet
for you are not finished yet
surely, the sun
will find me again
the radical hope too

and on the days when
i can't do anything but scream
and cry and dance at
this gift that has been
given to me, you shout
there is so much more
more of this gratitude
for complicated joys and
surprising blessings that
come after the battles
storms and hurts

the messy in-between

i used to pray that my life
would be perfect, but now
i pray that it will be
beautiful, honest
and real instead
i used to pray that every day
would be perfect, but now
i pray that each one
will be full of love, grace
and courage instead
i used to pray that i
would be perfect, but now
i pray that i can just be me
broken, human
and redeemed

-present over perfect

the messy in-between

send me to hard and dark places
the deepest of valleys
if that's what it takes
for me to be with you tonight
i just want to be with you tonight

-bold prayers

the messy in-between

sweet heart
dear friend
what have they done to you
how they have wronged you
scraped you raw
and broken you
how they have robbed you
of your hope

sweet heart
dear friend
there are no words for
the things you have seen
the pain you have carried
the heartbreak you have known
i now know the way
life hurts sometimes

my love, you are shrinking
before my very eyes
collapsing under the
weight of yourself and
what has happened to you
surely, this burden
is far too heavy for you
to carry all on your own

my love, i will carry it with you
your heart in one hand
mine in the other
until we find our way back home
surely, the road ahead of us is long
but you, the warrior, are brave
and who you are becoming
even more so

and dear
on the days
when you feel like
you have nothing left
inside of you but
your own broken heart
i will wrap you in my arms
and stay with you

my dear
i am opening the door
to my home
welcoming you in
pouring you a cup of tea
you will be safe here
make yourself at home
stay as long as you want

you soft and messy thing
no one knows how to love you
i will spend the rest of my days
learning how to love you
surely, the hurt will be real
and the road ahead of us long
but loving you is
all i ever want to do

you broken and beautiful thing
you are not alone
you never were
and never will be
do not beg me to leave you
i am not leaving you
i am not here to hurt you
i am here to love you

-a love letter to a beautiful and broken world

*inspired by "two" by sleeping at last

the messy in-between

you have spent
your entire life
terrified of yourself
and your potential

jumping at your
own shadow and
shaking at the sound
of your own voice

you are so desperate
not to look like your past
that you run
from your future

but you are not
what you have been
brought through
you are more

and you don't need
to look like those
that have hurt you
you are more

beloved, you don't need
to be scared anymore
for you are just you
and you are more

the messy in-between

and after all this time
i am sure of two things
and two things only
this world is broken
but it sure is beautiful
i am broken
but oh so loved

and this is how
i know what hope is
that just when
i think it is the end
it is only the beginning
broken is broken
but the sentence doesn't end there

and now, six months have passed
in this messy in-between
and the sun has set on
all kinds of human days
and you wouldn't believe
the things that i've seen
all that is to come

-broken and

the messy in-between

my heart breaks every time
the word *sorry* escapes your lips
you say you can't help it
but honey, tell me
where you learned you had
to apologize for the space
that you take up
where did you learn
that your own life
wasn't worth investing in
your own feelings
not worth listening to
where did you learn the lie
that you have to shrink
for them to love you
who taught you that
love was supposed
to hurt like this
honey, tell me
what i'm supposed to say
when *sorry* escapes your lips
one more time

-one more time

a beginner's guide to taking up space:

1. walk into every room like you own it.
2. give yourself permission to be where you are.
3. stop apologizing for having needs.
4. allow yourself to feel all your emotions.
5. tell the stories you have earned along the way.
6. extend the grace you give so freely to others to yourself.
7. accept love you cannot repay.
8. listen to your body and heart.
9. rest when you are tired.
10. believe that you are deserving of good things.

the messy in-between

these days
i am trying to make
my way back home
to a version of myself
that is only a millionth
of who i am

you ask me who she is

she is radiant
and wild and
incredibly alive
kind and hilarious
fearless and
unapologetic

she is who i am

but these days
the world has felt
more broken than whole
and i am beginning to
want to be anywhere
but where i am right now

you ask me who i am right now

and i say i am hurting
but hopeful
incredibly human
deep and complex
brave and
beautiful

that is who i am

and today, i will
no longer be confined
to *either or* but
instead *both and*
for i am all of those things
and more

i am who i am

and these days
i don't want to be anywhere
but where i am now
because it is enough
welcome to the
fullness of who i am

the fullness of who i am

the messy in-between

these days
i am not sure
why i am
the way that i am

the feeling
hurts far too much
to be a gift
i am not sure i want it

take it away from me
i beg as
he looks away
the silence is deafening

i lay awake at night
wondering if he knew
that life would hurt a little more
for someone like me

these days
i am not sure
why i am
the way that i am

-but i will learn to love her

the messy in-between

you tell me this
has been the plan all along
for my heart to break
just as yours did
i cannot help but think
what a cruel fate
between a rock
and a hard place
i find myself in
i never wanted this

it is becoming
harder and harder
to rise from here
the sun rises
only to mock me
shedding light on
the cracks of a heart
i once thought was
all the way healed
where is the grace here

there is a grace
that is present here
for even the
wastelands give way
to cool streams
and even the sun rises
on the hardest days
breaking what once was
breaking me open
into something new

and so i rise
stand at the crossroads
of hopeless and hopeful
with my once broken
and still broken heart
it is here
between a rock
and a hard place
that a flower blooms
in the waiting

*inspired by jacob zelinski

the messy in-between

insulation
is a lie
try as you might
nothing will protect you
from this life
nothing will prepare you
for the way it hurts sometimes
give your whole heart
or none of it
the heartbreak will find you
pushing, striving
and hustling aside
the sickness may come
the emptiness too
our hearts find hope
only to lose it again
there are no words for
the grief that has found you
the pain that feels all-consuming
even here, you are whole

heartbreak
is the reality
try as you might
sometimes your world
comes crashing down
and so i say to you
let it break
let your heart break
with the force of a thousand suns
vast, deep, and great
and let it be your something big
let it remind you of
where you've been
and how far you've come
let it be your battle cry
your survival guide
your *i made it and so can you*
your one loud *me too*
and the breaking of you
into something new

*inspired by jacob zelinski

the messy in-between

could it be that
you have been
preparing me
all this while
could it be that
you have been with me
through it all
send me through
the fire, the storm
the raging sea
wherever you go
i will follow
take me to the desert
and the land that flows
show me the mountaintops
and valleys
let these feet carry me
through the darkness
let these hands be open
as i climb this mountain
let this heart want
more than beauty but
an eternity of adventure

-eternity of adventure

the messy in-between

you and i
are a never-ending conversation
drawn out over
tea and quiet mornings
long drives
and big questions
stretches of road
one foot in front of the other
you are my greatest adventure
my first love
and sweetest hope
and though you are mysterious
silent when i demand you to be loud
you are present
you have never once left my side
you and i
are a never-ending conversation
in a lifetime of love

the messy in-between

the world has spoken
and it says
i will feel like this forever
for this is how it is
the halfway healing
the best case scenario

my God has spoken
and He says hope and
freedom is mine forever
for this is how He loves
full healing
the best case scenario

the world has spoken
and it says
i should just move on
for this is how it goes
life happens to us all
and i'm no exception

my God has spoken
and He says
i will rise again
for this is how it goes
new life given in full
i am the exception

the world has spoken
and it says
victim and slave
for this is how it will be
i am one or the other
sometimes both

my God has spoken
and He says
victor and free
for this is how it will be
i am one and the other
always both

the messy in-between

take it all away
strip me of all that i have
not all beautiful things
are meant to stay

take it all away
strip me of all that i have
the good was
never mine anyway

you give and
you take away
i count it
all as gain

i will climb
this mountain
place my idols
on the altar

as many times
as it takes
these hands are open
they raise to praise

take it all away
strip me of all that i have
not all beautiful things
are meant to stay

the messy in-between

here i am
at the terminal with
a broken heart in one hand
my duffel in the other
and here i am
home
but everything has changed
and i will never
be the same

here i am
on the road that i know
like the back of my hand
my duffel in the trunk
and here i am
on my way to you
but i do not know
where to begin and
where the tears end

the loss stings
the weight of grief
heavy still as i follow
the long, winding
path home to you
and i don't want
to cry anymore
because you are
coming home too

so i wipe my tears
and take two big breaths in
the weight of grief
heavy still as i find you
wishing that the
sweetness of now
would keep the
brokenness away for
just a little while longer

but this is real life
and though the sky is
painted cotton candy
and blue tonight
it will not stay that way
as much as i beg it to
and the sunsets
we're chasing don't
look like they used to

and it's been three
long, hard months
and we are finally
home
but i am not sure if
i recognize the eyes
that stare back at me
or the tears that
fall from my own

and here i am
at the table with
my broken heart
and your bursting one
and here we are
home
but everything has changed
and we will never
be the same

and here i am
on the road with
one hand on the wheel
my duffel in the trunk
and here i am
with you
but i do not know
where to begin and
where the grief ends

and i came to mourn
but you came to rejoice
and we do not know
where to start
or if we even do
tell me, do we laugh
or do we cry
do we dance or
do we pray first

do we fight
or should i just go
i have forgotten
how to love you and
you have forgotten
who you used to be
and i know they say
that there is a season
for everything

that we should rejoice
with those who rejoice
and mourn with those
who mourn
but i guess we never
really got it right
or learned how to do it
well enough
so maybe this is the place

where we walk away
from each other for the
things that we cannot be
to each other right now
and maybe this is the place
where we learn how
to cry and laugh
and pray and dance
all on our own

the messy in-between

and maybe one day
when the sky is painted
cotton candy and blue
we'll find our way back
to the beginning
learn how to celebrate
and grieve together
mourn and rejoice
all the way back home

the messy in-between

today, i woke up
and the sky had
turned a certain kind
of grey again
and i feel all kinds
of alone again as
the rain comes and
washes my joy away
the clouds grieve for
what they have lost
and i cry for what has
not yet been found
i cry, and i wonder
why the storm
has come back
and decided to stay
why the thunder booms
and lightning flashes
even on the sweetest
of summer days

i never wanted the wind
never asked for the waves
but here i find myself
on another stormy day
the darkness has settled
and the rain keeps
pouring down
but the worst part is over
the hope begins now
so here's to the dancing
to the singing in the rain
even when life gets a little messy
and is full of unexpected pain
here's to the heartbreak
and the heartache
the hope right here
in the messy in-between
the dancing
and the singing
even here in the rain

the messy in-between

these days
i am not sure
how much more
i can lose and
i feel afraid and
hopeless like before

it is becoming
harder and harder
to show up knowing
that you won't be right there
i never saw it coming
the end of you and me

but our paths
don't cross anymore
and we are entire worlds apart
what is there for us to do
when love doesn't feel
like enough anymore

but until it all
gets taken away
i need you to know
that if i had it my way
love would be
enough for us still

the messy in-between

we've been fighting
for months now
and just like sand
you are going
going, gone
and i feel out of control
like i cannot breathe
like i have already lost you
and will never know
anything as good

the messy in-between

and i will let the
past be the past
if you would give me
the answers
i have been begging for
for months on end

the messy in-between

i wept for the
first six months
after the day
you told me that
all that i was
wasn't enough for you
to want to stay anymore
i begged the heavens
for six months more
praying that
you loved me enough
to come back
when you were ready
and here i am
still waiting for that day

tell me again
how i was the worst thing
to happen to you
say those words
toxic and *manipulative*
one more time
how long did you drown for
and when did you begin
to feel like you had to choose
between me and God
tell me when i became the
monster i am not sure that i am
i say *tell me more* and
thank you for your honesty
as i memorize every syllable
replay our last conversation
on loop and fall to my knees
i repent for my sins and
handpick my apologies
choose my words carefully
all the poems in the world
could not save me from
who you think i am

and as the months pass
i learn how to crumble
at the loss one more time
i wonder if i am enough
if you see no worth in me
surely, there must be
none to be found
and if what you
are saying is true
then i want nothing
to do with the girl
that you have
decided that i am
she is far too broken
for anyone to love

tell me again
your words
remind me
that who i am
and how i love
aren't enough
i spend months
reeling from our
last conversation
your words are
where i return to
after a long day
i say *tell me more* and
thank you for your honesty
as i forget everything
beautiful i have ever
believed about myself
and learn to apologize for
ever daring to come as i was
loving the person i was becoming
all the poems in the world
and i am still learning that
who i am is enough

the messy in-between

and i promised myself
that i would never give anyone
the power to destroy me
but here you are
making it impossible
for me to love myself

and i wish i didn't always
worship at your feet
but here i am
bowing to your opinions
of who you think i am
once again

and i beg that your voice
would leave me
not become the
only story that i tell
but it is here
i am just me
and i am beloved

and this time
i will not worship
at your feet
i refuse to bow
your lies have no power here
i am standing on
firm rock now

the messy in-between

i am convinced
that i am the most
broken person i know
i reduce myself
to nothing just like
you taught me to

the messy in-between

and i lay awake at night
wondering if i am everything
they have decided that i am
and i do not want
to live a lie anymore
i am not who you think i am

you do not understand
this heart has been hurt
more than a couple times
and i am broken in
more ways than one
i am not always happy
and i hurt people sometimes
i am not who you think i am

and no, i do not want your praise
i am a little too broken for that
take it all back
for i am not the person
i want to be and
i am not worthy yet

-*yet*

the messy in-between

you convinced me
of my own goodness
had me believing
in love all over again
why did you build me up
only to tear me apart
take me this high
knowing it would all
come crashing down
why did you make me
love myself
only to pull the rug out
from under me

-self-hatred

the messy in-between

you must've known
you were breaking my heart
you must've known
how to make it hurt
you must've known
i would barely survive

-*but you did it still*

the messy in-between

and i want to let you go
but every poem i write
is about you and
every time the sun rises
i hope that it'll get easier
but it's getting harder
to forget you and
isn't it funny that
the grief still feels heavy
even though it's been months
since you walked out on us
and since you've been gone
my heart has wandered everyday
trying to make sense of
something that never will
and i do not know what else to do
because it has been decades
and i am still not over you
but i am so over grieving
and hurting like this
tell me why i still love you
when all i know is hurt
tell me how to fix this broken heart
and how to get over losing a friend

the messy in-between

and i want to forget you
but i am still haunted
by the memories of
who we once were
and i want you to be
happy, but i am not
sure i know how to be

and these days
i am learning that
sometimes love changes
even when you never asked it to
and sometimes, people
can't stay even when
they promised they would

so i will learn how
to grieve this loss
and grow from it
and i will learn how
to let the people
that can no longer
love me beautifully
walk away now

the messy in-between

how long did
your heart ache
for what once was
when you called me that day
your voice was shaking too
surely, neither of us
could face the truth
of what came next

the messy in-between

if i let myself feel
i would never
stop missing you

the messy in-between

and what kills me
more than anything
is that you seem
happier after it all
and after it all
i am still devastated
and i guess
i have been healing
but it takes too long
and hurts too much
to be real

the messy in-between

does your heart
still cry out for me
in the middle of the night
we are kindred spirits
i hurt as you do
and that is how i know
you aren't okay too

the messy in-between

please do not
be cruel
i miss when
you were soft
and gentle

the messy in-between

i gave you all the love
i had to give
and it still wasn't enough
and that will always hurt

the messy in-between

you are not my
best friend anymore

the messy in-between

you are not who
i thought you were

the messy in-between

you took everything from me
even my self-love
the trust i had built
between me and myself
when everything in me
told me to leave
when you didn't seem
to mind hurting me
i let you rewrite the story
and decide the ending

-never again

the messy in-between

you never reacted
when i wept at your feet
you never showed up
when you said that you were sorry
you never fought for us
when all i wanted was
my best friend back

the messy in-between

i have spent the
last nine months
letting you convince me
that i am nothing
and i have spent the better
half of this year crawling
out of my grave after you

the messy in-between

i am afraid to heal
because the drowning
is all i know
ask me, and i'd still choose
the hurt over the
freedom any day
and i am afraid to be happy
because it means
i am moving on
and i am not ready
to be just like you yet

-*indifferent*

the messy in-between

another hard week
passes me by
and i would be lying
to you if i said
i didn't feel tired
lonely and afraid sometimes
and i promise
i am fighting hard
wishing people saw me clearly
but i am too tired
lonely and afraid
for this again
and they always
tell me that they love me
but leave when they can
and they always
tell me that there is all
the grace in the world for me
but they always
forget to give it to me
and so i am left
feeling a long way
from home
numb and lost
as another hard week
passes me by

the messy in-between

the voices are loud
the shame and regrets too
as i lay awake fighting them
i guess we all find a way
of distorting the people we love
reducing them to shadows
we know they are not

the messy in-between

i think about it all often
and hardly a day
passes me by
when i don't miss you
it seems silly
to want something that
doesn't want me anymore
to ask love to stay
when all it knows
is how to leave

they say it's for the better
but i haven't gotten
to that part quite yet
and they say that
all is fair in love and war
but i'm still figuring out
which one this is
and i wonder if
you would still be here
if i was less broken

the messy in-between

i have crawled
on my hands and knees
through the wilderness
desperate for answers
begging for healing
that did not want to come
but still did, and even
when the victory
hid its face from me
i learned how to
speak gently to
myself again

the messy in-between

there were times
i could not see
my own growth
i had convinced myself
healing meant it
didn't hurt anymore
but the grief could
not be so easily shaken
overnight and over time
overstaying its welcome

and here we are
nearly a year later
and i do not think
i have given myself
enough credit for
growing all the while
for healing through
the hurt and choosing
to move forward in
the face of grief

the messy in-between

the grief is enormous
sometimes a dull ache
other times a roaring pain
and it has been almost a year
since we first began to unravel
and it all fell apart
and it still hurts like hell
sometimes a dull ache
other times a roaring pain
but so it goes
life happens to us all
and we learn how to
survive it somehow

the messy in-between

it has been a lifetime
since i last looked
into your eyes
i trade sunrise for sunset
and hard day
for harder night

and while i still have
so many questions
and not enough answers
i can tell that i have
been healing all the while

and we found heaven
in bits and pieces
of feeling alright
and love, hope, and joy
on this journey
grace-filled and lined

the messy in-between

i woke up this morning
with a lightness in my soul
the garden continues to grow
even when you are not here
tell me the lies one more time
i'll dance in the truth of who i am
for the rest of my life
you don't get a say
you don't get to tell me that who i am
and how i love are not enough
when i am sure that they are

the messy in-between

i am not sure
where you are at these days
if we were to meet again
you would have to
introduce me
to who you are
all over again
would my body remember
you or the pain
how i missed you
or hated myself
would i fall to the floor
heart stuck in my throat
would i run to you
or would i finally learn
how to let you go

-for the last time

the messy in-between

i saw you for
the first time
in what felt like
an eternity
you turned around
and smiled
you look happy
don't you now
and every time
i have seen you
my heart has hurt the same
but this time
i managed to smile back
because i am
happy now too

the messy in-between

i wonder if you think
about me sometimes
i wonder if you would
tell me if you weren't happy
and i wonder if i would
still rush to your side
like i always said i would
i wonder if i would
have enough strength
to hold it all
but i have always loved you
far more than the brokenness
you call home
and i think i'd want to be
right there with you
even if i couldn't do it well

the messy in-between

let's dance even on the days
it doesn't make sense
when there's no music
and life is one big mess

let's pray even on the nights
the tears come and decide to stay
when there are no words
and i am begging you to stay

let's talk on the drives
that stretch on for days
when there is nothing but road
and unspoken hurt between us

let's laugh on the adventures
we take, the places we go
when there is nothing but us
and this big, beautiful world

let's scream even when
the world demands us to be quiet
when a whisper isn't loud enough
and what we've built is worth fighting for

let's run even if
it's just in circles
when we don't have it all figured out
and nothing is guaranteed

let's love even when
it's the hardest thing
especially when it's the hardest thing
let's love all the more

the messy in-between

i cannot bring myself
to blame you
for any of it
you are too worthy
of grace for me
to feel anything
but hope
it still hurts, yes
i miss you all the time
but if you peel back
all of the layers
i am still struggling
to let go of the person
that i once knew
if you brought them back to me
i would run to them
with arms wide open
i wonder if i am naive
to want you back
foolish to welcome love
that heals and hurts
all in the same breath

the messy in-between

the year comes and goes
and i learn to
forgive myself
for loving you
with all that i had
all of the songs
make sense to me now
there is no distance
you could go that
would stop me from
running to you still

-*prodigal son*

the messy in-between

i thought i was
loving you but
i know better now

the messy in-between

i think i really loved you
and i am learning how
to forgive myself now

the messy in-between

the grief comes in waves
never stays long enough
for me to claim as my own
ebbs and flows
for months on end
and one whole year later
it begins to sting a little less
every time i think
i miss you the same but
we are entirely different people now
aren't we
and in the space left between us
i dare to learn about
this thing called love
the nuances and intricacies of it
how it still exists
even when two people
walk away from each other
how it is so much
bigger than i thought
how sometimes it looks
like grief when you care

the messy in-between

dear friend,

we still love you. we miss you every day. if you came back to us, our arms would be wide open. i wonder if you even know the grace that is for you. do you want it, or do you need to be away for a little while longer. would you tell us if you weren't happy. would you come back if you weren't. will the highs last forever. how long did you drown for. is this who you are, or did it hurt you too. are you lost, or are you freer than ever. how will we ever know the difference. how many more days will we go on like this. with no closure and not enough honesty. we thought you'd want to stay. that you'd be here with us now. that we'd still be seen by the person that saw us so well. all these months later, and we still miss you. we love you too much to not want you to come back to us soon.

the messy in-between

and so you left
and built a new life
for yourself that did
not have room for me

and so here i stand
fighting to love the life
that is still left for me
to live after you

and here i stand
on the corner
where you told me
you didn't want to stay

an old photograph in one hand
my broken heart in the other
wondering where it
all went so wrong

and i do not want
to forget what once
was beautiful
and good

but i am having
trouble remembering
what this duet
sounded like

and i wish i could
turn back time to remind
myself that we haven't
always been this way

i think we were
really happy once
before it all
got torn apart

and i'd give anything
to have it all back
but maybe my life can still
be beautiful without you

and maybe nothing
can take away
from what i thought
was good and pure

even if it doesn't stay
and so i will stand
on this corner
where it all fell apart

and hold these
old photographs up high
on display for the
whole world to see

and i will tell them
my story of redemption
unfolding in real time and
a little frayed around the edges

and i will tell them
all about you
all the late nights and
long drives smiling at me

and when the years
have passed and
i cannot remember
who we once were

i will pull out these
photo albums and
celebrate what once
was beautiful and good

*inspired by judah & the lion

the messy in-between

and while i may never know
why you couldn't stay
i hope i can still stand up
at the end of the day
and say to you
thank you for your part
in my full and still
unfolding redemption
my heart is forever
slanted towards love
and try as you might
i am not going anywhere
this heart can't do
anything but love

the messy in-between

i understand why you had to leave
it wasn't healthy for you to stay anymore
with the codependency and idolatry
i loved to play rescuer
and you were always drowning
my pride and ego got the best of me
and i lost all control
my whole self
in the need to protect you
we called it love
but i think i had it wrong
love wasn't walking away
when you wanted space
love wasn't giving up
when you had already decided to
love wasn't letting you feel alone
when you needed to be on your own
love wasn't any boundaries
and come as you are
i think i had love
some kind of wrong
but i didn't know any better
i really thought i was loving you
i think i still do
but i get why you had to leave now

-*sometimes the why comes later*

the messy in-between

to the friend i lost,

i love you, but i don't want to fight anymore. i am sorry for all the pain and confusion that i caused. i forgave you a long time ago. over a year later, i understand the "why" now. i understand in more ways than one. and so i will walk away for the both of us. i miss you, but i just can't stay anymore. there is a world of hurt between us, one that might not be reconciled on this side of eternity. but my heart knew love and community with you, and my heart is learning how to let you go now too.

the messy in-between

and i do not want
to be afraid
but every time
i dare to hope in love
it falls apart
in front of my eyes
and i want you to stay
but the door is that way
take your time
make sure it hurts
stay for a little while
know my whole heart
and next time
you love someone
make sure you mean it

the messy in-between

and all i've wanted all this time
was a love that would stay
but that is the one thing
you couldn't commit yourself to
loving me in a kind way

the messy in-between

everything in my mind
is still tangled from
the time we tried
to love each other

-*gaslighting*

the messy in-between

i still shake
from the time that
i let you tell me
who i was

the messy in-between

why do you run
from love that is
gentle and sweet

why do you push
people away, only to
pull them back in again

why do you feel
the need to break me
just because you can

why do you control
and manipulate
when you know
that i will stay

the messy in-between

i have seen it for myself
i know all the signs
they have all kinds of words
for people like you
for so long, i needed
to know exactly
what they were
so i could string
them together and
make sense of it all

first, they forced me
to make you
into a monster
i knew you were not
in order to heal
second, they told me
it was all a lie
that you didn't love me
that you never did
that you never could

but maybe it was all real
the abuse and the love
the good and the hell
and maybe i can still learn
how to trust myself
and how i felt
maybe i loved you
and it broke my heart
and maybe i can learn
how to love myself now

the messy in-between

i shy away from
the compliment
one more time
i have been taught
to shrink from what
has always been mine
and i do not want
your opinion of me
it is full of lies
i am not who you think i am
and so i will keep your words
locked away in a box
save it for a rainy day
but if what you say is true
then i will learn it
for myself one day

the messy in-between

and if i am being honest
i feel so unworthy
of everything you have to give
how can you love me
when i am this painfully human

the messy in-between

i weep again
i am so tired
of being broken
of dragging this
heart-sized hole around
wherever i go
trauma and triggers
anxiety and anger
how do i leave them
behind in my past
where they belong

the messy in-between

i don't want to be broken anymore
it hurts far too much to ever want
tell me how to make it easier
i want to be perfect now

i don't want to be broken anymore
tell me how to be good like her
i try to fix myself, but the books
and potions are never enough

i don't want to be broken anymore
there is still so much work to get done
i lose myself in the name of growth
learn to punish myself for all that i'm not

i don't want to be broken anymore
i've been for far too long
and the cost is far too high
i lose everything that i've ever loved

i don't want to be broken anymore
because all i seem to do is hurt people
i am so tired of hurting you
in the name of love

i don't want to be broken anymore
this journey is far too messy
give me the easy and the pretty
i just want to arrive

i don't want to be broken anymore
because it means that the voices
have been right all along
i am unworthy of love

i don't want to be broken anymore
because i am afraid of
what i might discover
about myself along the way

i don't want to be broken anymore
because i am afraid of
my own need and humanness
i don't want to be just like them

i don't want to be broken anymore
because it means that
i am imperfect and human
and still worthy of love

the messy in-between

from the moment
my eyes open to
greet the morning sun
the questions plague me
who am i and
what have i done
i lay in bed paralyzed
by my worst fears
trapped as a victim
of my own mind
the grief always comes
in the morning
it knows how to find me
before the day even begins

the messy in-between

i have read all the articles
and self-help books
and i still cannot tell
who broke who first
tell me the difference between
the victim and the abuser
how do i know which one i am
if i've made mistakes too

what does it say about me
that i have always been whole
and i have only continued to
love you long after you've gone
does it mean anything
that i grieved you for years
learned to hate myself
because of your words
am i playing victim
or was it not my fault
the line is too blurry
and i am too imperfect still
but i think i am human
and we fell out of love

the messy in-between

i am still recovering
from the abuse
i used to believe in love
but not anymore

i wait for you to walk away
i've heard these lies before
it is all the same
no one ever stays

i let myself be loved once
but all it did was break my heart
i learned that love hurts
when you let it in sometimes

i learn to hate who i am
i cannot forgive myself
for all that i've done
i reject the praise that comes

i ask people to stay
feel unsafe in my own mind
convince myself that i am unworthy
of love and trust all the time

-relational trauma

the messy in-between

i can't tell if i'm
reliving the same story
or writing a new one

the messy in-between

it has been years
but i cannot outrun
what has been broken
i cannot undo
what you have done
to my mind
how did you turn
the safest place i knew
into a cold abyss
there are so many words
still left unspoken
how do i heal from
all that i lost that day
i grieve you for months
want you back more
than i need myself
to be okay again
i dream of you
and wake up in tears
i cannot erase the
lies of the abuse
i've tried, but i cannot
outrun the likes of you

the messy in-between

i begin the healing work
many years after you
time passes, but the trauma
demands to be felt still

for many months
i cannot bring myself
to say the words out loud
abuse sits idly on my tongue

i convince myself
out of every emotion
perform gymnastics and
surgery on my own mind

i wonder if what
i'm feeling is real
i jump through hoops
learn to remove the truth

maybe after it all
it wasn't that bad
and maybe i deserved
everything that i got

you're right
it was all my fault
just like last time
i'm sorry again

am i making this all up
i run to my friends
but they all tell me that
i'm being dramatic again

i cannot remember
what i came here to
tell you in the first place
maybe that i deserve more

but you're right
surely, i am too broken
to be worthy of
anything else

i wonder if there is
more to life than this
my mind has not been
my own for so long

tell me which way
back to the self-love
i want none of the
hate that you give

it has taken me years
but i am here now
the truth finds its way in
and i begin to heal

the messy in-between

and life is beautiful
but i still feel numb
to it all somehow
my heart is restless
begs for purpose
a relief from it all
where is the full life
all my friends talk about
i can't tell if i need
more grace or honesty
i forget how to listen to my body
the connection fades
and i run ashamed
this is not the life
that i wanted after all
and i want to come
but i am afraid to
be seen by you now
am i a year too late
tell me which way
back to your arms
and to the full life
that was promised to me

the messy in-between

your words follow me
everywhere i go
i cannot shake the
voices inside my head
the lies spread like a cancer
faster than my mind
can comprehend
anxiety is a prison
within the walls of my own skin
i am gasping for air
stuck somewhere
between breathing
and drowning
my mind wanders
betrays and replays
our last conversation
how did i end up
crumpled on the
kitchen floor like this
my knees give way
my hands shake as i rise
and beg for mercy
for relief from
the weight of you

-*anxiety*

the messy in-between

what if grace is
enough for everybody
but me, and the
gospel is not good
news for everyone

what if i am not ready
to hold the tensions
of a big, messy world
what if i never find
the healing that i have
been fighting for

what if i miss you always
what if i trusted you
with all that i had
and all you did was
break me again

what if the weight
of the world is
always mine to hold
what if it is too heavy
and i want to lay it down
for a little while

what is complacency
and what is grace
how do i learn
how to fail when
all i know is shame

what is justice and
who is the gospel for
who can hold the tensions
of a broken world well
and who am i when you
aren't around anymore

do you ever think
of me sometimes
does it hurt you
like it hurts me
when you are alone

is there rest
and grace for me
in a world that
constantly demands
more and more
from my weary soul

-*questions*

the messy in-between

trying harder has always been
the answer to the question
am i seen, known, and loved
do more and do better
is all i've ever known

the messy in-between

i have scraped myself dry
looking for answers
that do not come easily
tell me, if i clench
my fists and
wish it all away
would it make me
less broken

and what if there
is no relief for
all that i have done
and grace is enough
for everyone but me
what happens if the
well runs dry and
spits me out whole

-lies

the messy in-between

grace
you look nothing
like i imagined
you are softer
harder around the edges
you look like
the sins i repent for
in the dead of night

if you only knew
that i am not
who they think i am
you would walk away too
but here you are
refusing to let the lies
take what was never
theirs in the first place

and i do not understand
why you haven't
kept a record of
all that i have done
tell me why
there is only love
in your eyes
after all this time

and i am used to
keeping secrets
don't say you love me
or i will run
like i always do
but you are pulling me
towards you
insisting that i stay

and i do not deserve you
have not earned
what you so freely give
give me some time
and a repentant heart
and maybe i can
still find my way
back home to you

grace
you make no sense to me
you should have left
like the others did
all those years ago
i have no words
for you, but a weary
world rejoices

as i freefall into
a love i still
do not understand
all i know is that
i need you now
and i have tried
to do this alone
for far too long

and it is here that
a lifetime of earning
and failing is edged out
by all that you are
it is here that i find
that you have been
for me all along
it is here that grace is enough

-*grace changes everything*

the messy in-between

you take my fear
and turn it into dancing
you take my hand
and tell me that i'm never alone
you take my worst mistake
and say come as you are

the messy in-between

you take what is broken
dead and gone
breathe new life into it
and call it hope

the messy in-between

you take my worst mistake and
turn it into your greatest victory

the messy in-between

when you have
lost everything and
the end feels near
please know
that your story
is far from over

-*the best is yet to come*

the messy in-between

even on the days
that it still hurts
may we have the courage
to grieve enough
and on the days
we feel fragile and undone
may we remember
our grief may not
know a timeline
but the healing
still comes

-one year anniversary

the messy in-between

and i guess
even here
grace is still abundant
flowing freely like
the rivers in your soul
and it is here
that you will learn
the unforced rhythms of grace
pushing and pulling you
towards the healing
that has always been yours

inspired by matthew 11:28-30

the messy in-between

even here, i am whole
in my heartbreak and anxieties
my greatest insecurities
and biggest questions
when i barely have
the strength to rise
i will rise

-and i will be whole

the messy in-between

even here, you are loved
even here, you are held
even here, you are enough
even here, you are whole

the messy in-between

those three words alone
bring me to my knees
i cannot stop crying
i do not want any part of what comes next
i hear the invitation again
but the last time it hurt too bad
after you, i haven't been able
to let love in again

the castle i have built
the moat surrounds me now
no one can enter
or leave
the walls are high
and the tower is empty
the drawbridge isn't lowering
even though the people are knocking

those three words
can't possibly be true
they tell me i'll know love again
but it never comes
i cannot bring myself
to hope after you
i shut down in order
to save myself

the castle i have built
keeps me safe
gives my heart time to heal
your eyes are kind
but i am already gone
i have known you in another life
but we are not accepting
visitors right now

those three words
are all that i've ever wanted
but not what i've known
i receive love, but it
never feels like enough
i give all of myself
but don't know how to
accept love when it comes

the castle i have built
is the only way to protect
my fragile heart
i have been taught
i need to work harder
to earn love, but
somehow i feel just
as alone as before

those three words
are changing everything now
i do not feel ready
but i think i want to try
to open my heart again
a part of me hopes that
i have been worthy of
good love all this time

the castle i have built
is starting to crumble now
the moat is filled and
the tower comes crashing down
as i raise a white flag of surrender
the drawbridge lowers as
i learn to let love in
one more time

-*let love in*

the messy in-between

to anybody that is grieving something in this season that they're not ready to talk about yet:

i hope you know that you can take your time. that your process is sacred and valuable. before it makes sense. and even when it still hurts. only you know the way back home, and you are allowed to ask for what you need as you go. i know it's hard, i know your heart is so broken. i know you are tired. so tired.

i am sorry that you have had to carry this alone for so long. it is too much for one person to bear. we want to carry it with you now. you have come such a long way already. we are proud of you for trying, for showing up, for fighting in the ways you can. we are here now, and you are safe. we can't take the pain away, oh how we wish we had the words. but you can take your time healing. and if you need us, we will be here.

the messy in-between

beloved
we are proud of you
for taking the time
you need to heal
we hope that you know
we love you and always will

and we know that you are afraid
we can hear it in your voice
the hurt and the longing
for grace you don't deserve
but that voice also carries strength
and all the hope in the world

and for all that fell apart
without an explanation
you still dare to see the good
you have loved hard
and fought harder, lost love
you thought would stay

and for all that was
never your fault
we have been with you
through it all
we hear you and we see you
we have never left your side

we believe you
and we trust you
what the world says aside
you are allowed to be loved
right here and right now
before it's all figured out

and while you are still broken
afraid of getting it wrong
or of having never
gotten it right
you are allowed
to forgive yourself

and you are allowed
to trust yourself
for as long as there is
breath in your lungs
you can still be good
it's okay that it's messy

it's okay that you're human
you are allowed to
see your own worth
through the confusion
and the grief
you are enough

and i know that you are
doing the best you can
though your heart has
been through so much
you have never once
given up on love

and i hope that you know
through it all
you are allowed
to grow and love
who you are becoming
right here and right now

-home team

the messy in-between

you wrap me
in the word *together*
in the truth that
we were not made
to do this alone
that we will survive
this imperfectly and
by each other's sides

the messy in-between

we are getting
lost on this path
weaving between
heartbreak and hope
the sun sets on our backs
but we have not
stopped chasing it
the light
it follows us wherever we go
it fights to stay
a quarter past
and the whole town
is still on fire
freefalling into hope
as the light fades and
we chase sunsets again

the messy in-between

you drove all the way
to my house
because you heard
that i felt alone
and there's a drink
sitting on my doorstep
and an old friend
standing on my porch
we lay on the sidewalk
and you ask me how i am
and what hurts these days
and we begin to grieve together
hands stretched high
one act of surrender
and rebellion
stories are shared
and tears fall
in my neighbor's front yard
and the healing we have
always wanted finds its way in
even the darkness of the night
cannot contain the light between us
as we dance and celebrate
pray like we've never prayed before
and just like that
life is beautiful again

the messy in-between

you are a breath
of fresh air
as the world
gasps for oxygen

-*unsung heroes*

the messy in-between

you are not a mistake
you are not a mistake
you are not a mistake

the messy in-between

it has been an
especially trying year
hasn't it, my friend
for you have loved and lost
all in the same day
you say the grief
does not go down easy
we just learn how to live
with a broken heart
but i can see you
carrying yourself through
all the way in the dark
and though the night comes early
and tries to make a home here
you refuse to back down that easy
with that big, beautiful
and broken heart of yours
and i trust that it will
just keep on beating
because we made a promise
from the start
a promise that we'd keep living
even with a broken heart

-to cindy

the messy in-between

and on the days
your world
comes screeching
to a standstill and
the bravest thing
that you can do
is get out of bed
take four deep breaths in
and another five out
and know that you
do not need to be
anything grand today
no, you can be little
and you can be scared
you can carry grief
and all of your cares

somewhere along the way
you will find this world
does not need you to be grand
just honest
and it will keep spinning until
life feels worth living again
and in the waiting
you do not need to be perfect
you do not need to know what comes next
for God delights in small beginnings
and your beginning is coming yet
take all the time you need to rest easy
to pace yourself for the journey ahead
take four deep breaths in and
know that all that you have
is grand enough for today

the messy in-between

dear friend,

tell me your story of heartbreak
and i'll tell you mine
we have both lived some
beautiful and real life, haven't we
and when we have run out of words
i will learn how to sit on the floor
and weep with you
and when all is said and done
i will say what a beautiful privilege
it is to love, even when
it breaks your heart sometimes

the messy in-between

dear me,

there are no easy answers
for the *why*s
you wrestle with in the dead of night
but i have seen you show up
bravely all the while
and i have been watching you
for some time now
seeing how you fight
to believe you're enough
even when the lies are loud
and they make you doubt yourself
you refuse to let them
stop you from loving yourself

the messy in-between

i refuse to fight
for love that does
not want to stay

-for a single second longer

the messy in-between

i miss the way
i believed in the
love that i gave
when you were here

but you are not
why i loved
the way that i did
you just happened
to be the recipient

the messy in-between

you tried to tear me down
as if your words could
make me less of what
i have always been

if my identity is
not earned but given
how could you
possibly take it away

-*beloved*

the messy in-between

and while it is true that
i will not always know
how to love the eyes
that stare back at me
i will spend the rest
of my days trying
guessing and asking
failing big and
falling short
time and time again

and i will not be
ashamed of the heart
inside of me that beats
to love you extravagantly
and i will not water down
the story that carries
the words to my healing
i will not fight the song
rising up inside of me
the poetry that flows from me

and while it is true that
i will not always know
how to love the eyes
that stare back at me
i want to spend the rest
of my days trying anyways

and yes, it is true
i am still broken
and i am still
figuring this all out
but i will spend the rest
of my days learning
growing and fighting
failing big and
falling short
time and time again

and i will not be
ashamed of the cracks
inside of my heart
where the light gets in
and i will not apologize
for this testimony
that i get to live and
i will not fight against
the person God made me to be
at the end of the day, she's just me

and while it is true that
i am still broken
and i am still
figuring it all out
i want to spend the rest
of my days trying anyways

the messy in-between

you are not hurting anyone
you are just you
and that is enough

-*the words i needed to hear*

the messy in-between

i want to love you
but i am afraid
of hurting you
i don't want
to hurt you like
i hurt everyone else

but the deeper the love
the higher the cost
do we risk it all or
do we give up now
do we convince ourselves
out of good things or
do we let ourselves
be worthy of love
and belonging again

the messy in-between

and i have been
begging you to
teach me who i am
but it is me that must
learn how to love myself
and i will be the first to say
that i do not know
where to start
where your opinion ends
and i begin
and i am lonely
afraid that this journey
will take everything from me
that the hole inside my heart
is too deep to heal
but i want to learn to love
who i am becoming
so let us begin walking
this road less taken
all the way back home

the messy in-between

and because we will
not always have
someone to hold us
in the middle of the night
we must learn how to
be that person for ourselves
to love the body
that lays with us
and for all the times
people let us down
we must learn how to
let ourselves be enough
and when the world
tries to convince us otherwise
we must learn how to
get on the floor and
pull poetry out
of our stories and
write love letters
to the hurt and
when we are alone
we must learn to speak
to ourselves kindly
gently like an old friend
and if nothing else
we must learn how
to love ourselves first

the messy in-between

i have never met
anything like you
when he said *quiet*
you say *tell me more*
when he ran away
you run towards
when he couldn't love
you love all the more

the messy in-between

i think you
are the dream
i have never
let myself believe

-the one

the messy in-between

whoever loves you
will be full for
the rest of their life

the messy in-between

tell me what the world
looks like from your eyes
is it beautiful
is it full of awe and wonder
does it make you
want to dance
they say you have
not lived enough life
to understand it
but i think you have
lived just enough life
to not miss it
and i want to know
your beautiful world
will you teach me
how to dance again

the messy in-between

and i thought i knew
what love was
but i guess it looks
a little different
than i thought
so i will start
from the beginning
as many times
as it takes

-drawing board

the messy in-between

and *love*
you are beautiful
i will spend the rest of my life
learning and unlearning you
but when you hurt
please remind me that
you can be soft and gentle too

the messy in-between

how can i trust in something
that never stays even
when it promises it will

the messy in-between

get too close
and i will run
as i always do
i want none
of comes next

-the possibility of love

the messy in-between

i do not know how
to make it better
i have given all
of myself to an
unforgiving master

i want to love you
but i don't know
how to trust myself
and my messed up
ideas of love

i do not know how
to make it better
it breaks my heart
every single time
i can't get it right

i want to love you
but all i seem to do
is make things worse
i didn't come here to
break both of our hearts

-*yet here i am*

the messy in-between

tell me. where you learned how to give good and healthy love. i only ask because i am not convinced i know how. when the people who are supposed to teach you cannot, you must look elsewhere. did you learn it from them, or did they yell and scream too. did you find it already, or do you still search for it in a stranger's eyes. did someone help you come home to yourself, or are you still undoing their trauma from your mind. i wonder if i know what love is. if i am even capable of it. if i would recognize it if it came to me now. if i would run like i always do. i wonder how many more days will pass before i have all the answers to my questions. how many more people will i hurt. how much longer like this. broken and searching. am i a product of my past, or the future i am reimagining for myself. am i more than my mistakes, or am i bound to repeat everything that has been done to me. tell me. where you learned how to give good and healthy love. is it okay that i am still learning how.

the messy in-between

i fall to my knees
one more time
my past lays tired
at my feet
a broken record
on repeat
a broken record
on repeat
someone tell me
how to get the abuse
out of my bloodstream
how do i love again
when they pulled poems
and whole stories out of me
earned my trust
only to betray me
made me feel not alone
finally had me believing
in myself again
only to break me
like a record

-*broken records*

the messy in-between

i fall to my knees
and learn how to
love myself again
a tug-of-war and
battle i am not sure
i know how to win

the messy in-between

my heart breaks
under the weight
of an aching world
the complicated joy of
learning how to love you well
the need to fix you became me
i cannot sleep when you are like this
i am sure that i love you
too much to leave
i cannot turn away
your worst doesn't scare me
tell me what hurts and
how to make it all better
months pass and
i lose touch with who i am
we are not who we used to be
and i am beginning to realize
that i cannot fix you

as much as i try
i only reach the end of myself every time
i thought if i just loved you enough
i could somehow make it all better
but learning to love you
might look a little different
than i thought, and so
i will continue to find my own limits
face my brokenness
knowing that there are some things
that are not mine to carry
the weight of you, certainly not
but the love that i feel
letting it be enough
i lay down my own ideas of love
and ask instead to be taught real love
i cannot fix you, but i want to
learn how to love you now

the messy in-between

i am not here to hurt you
i am here to love you
but i am human, so i will
get it a little wrong sometimes
but i hope the way
that i choose to love will
still be enough for you today

-the way that you choose to love is enough

the messy in-between

i wake up every morning
and beg the heavens to
teach me how to love you
oh, how i wish
i had more of myself
to give to you now

oh, how i wish
i could stay with you
for a little while longer
tell me what hurts and
what the grief feels like
how is your heart these days

oh, how i wish
i wasn't so tired
and that there was
enough to go around
but time is the one thing
i never have enough of

and yes, i still see you
even after all this time
i did not leave you then
and i will not leave you now
i still love you even as
we're figuring this out

and it is here that i must
rest and regain my strength
i can't tell you how long
it will take me, but
i promise i'm trying
to love you these days

and i wish i had more
of myself to give
but i guess all i can do
is ask for grace as
i learn how to love you
imperfectly today

the messy in-between

i hope that worthiness
and kindness would
find you in the face
of all things unknown
and still lost

the messy in-between

i want to pick you up
hold you close
until i understand
you more fully
if you are anything
you are a gentle teacher
a kind reminder
of my broken
and fragile heart
come now and stay
if you are here now
i ask that you
have your way
if i must know you
to surrender you
then let it be so
i will not label you
as good or bad
you are allowed to
come as you are too

-*a love letter to my emotions*

the messy in-between

heartbreak is a
small price to pay
for a live lived
wholeheartedly

the messy in-between

let us be people
that never grow tired
of asking people
how we can
love them well

the messy in-between

and i have decided
i am madly in love
with this gloriously
messy life of mine
and i have decided
i wouldn't want it
any other way
and i have decided
to keep being brave today

the messy in-between

and just like that
life is beautiful again
yet i am discovering
that it always has been

the messy in-between

and after everything has been said and done, i am thankful for it all. so give it up for complicated joys and a beautiful life i wouldn't trade for the world.

-*lessons around the sun*

the messy in-between

when you were here
i was a poet
but when you had left
i became a ghost

the messy in-between

years later
i find the words
to the love story
that changed my life

the messy in-between

when i was born
a generational curse
was placed on my shoulders
break the cycle
they told me
this world will swallow
you whole if you let it

the world is watching
waiting for you to fail
prove every single one
of them wrong
if scarcity is my birthright
i will dare to live
abundantly all the more

the whirlpool cannot touch us
where the oceans once
carried us to shore
my submission could not
be found in my revolution
they wanted to silence me
but all i did was find my voice

my life has always been
an epic love story
bursting with generations of revolt
they taught me that
survival is the most
sacred act of resistance
how we break the cycle

the messy in-between

they first tried to
suppress my voice
but they could not turn
a mighty force
into a gentle whisper
no one told me revolution
tasted like poetry
my voice is sacred
it may shake
but always demands more
it holds pain and depth
a lifetime spent in the messy
the greys of the in-between
it speaks desperately and urgently
i inhale deeper to fill my lungs
with all the sweet softness of my words
wonderful, tender, honest
love letters to the world
i will speak my own liberation
into existence
if revolution is what you want
it is here now

the messy in-between

things to remember as you continue to heal:

1. take a couple of deep breaths.
2. it's okay that it still hurts.
3. you carry the burden of something that doesn't have forever written on it.
4. the work is not finished. you have yet to see the end of this love story.
5. the heartbreak will not get the final say. you will soften and harden under love again.
6. your softness is your greatest strength. your humanness is a gift.
7. when you have nothing left, hope anyway.
8. you have come a long way, and you are loved.

the messy in-between

how have i never seen it until now
everything i have ever wanted
has been right here
within myself
could it be that you have
loved me all this time
have i always been good
i thought they had taken
everything from me
but it turns out that
i have been beloved
worthy and enough
my whole life

the messy in-between

what a long way i have come
and what a gift this journey has been
through it all, i am sure that
my God is not finished yet
i have taken one step at a time
let the healing come
found what was lost
and decided it is well

the messy in-between

it's been one hell
of a journey
but i am here now
different, better
more resilient
joyful in a new way
free in a real way
braver, stronger
more nuanced

the messy in-between

i stop to take in the view
i used to feel so alone
but i am safe now
and i am healing still

the messy in-between

the sun rises and passes
mountains thrown
into the sea
and you have been
growing all this time
since when did you become
so full all on your own
since when did you know love
since when did you find joy
somewhere in this
messy in-between

inspired by mark 11:22-23

the messy in-between

the words find me slowly
in the messy in-between
the poems come to me gently
in the darkness and in the sun
over the years, i watch myself
begin to heal and grow
learn to love and pick myself up
as many times as it hurts
and when all has been said and done
i think that love looks a
little different than i thought
is more beautiful and full
has always been mine

love heals quietly
does not cause anxiety
always seeks to understand
always chooses in
love does not punish or withhold
make us hate ourselves
love knows how to be alone
makes sure you are whole
love does not try
to be more than it is
love is safe and brave
feels like coming home
builds trust and hope
wants to stay and
heals more than it hurts

*inspired by 1 corinthians 13:4-8

the messy in-between

i know you did all you could
i know the voices growing up
all screamed bad news
i am sorry that it hurt
like that for so long
i am sorry that i couldn't
make it all better
i am sorry that you tried
to break free from your past
only to relive it again
it is not your fault
you couldn't help but live
the story they wrote for you
i know you did not mean
for it to be like this
sometimes the trauma
changes us in ways
we never wanted
so you've hurt people
haven't we all
so you're a little broken
you're not the only one
you are more than
your worst mistakes and bad days
and try as you might
you're just not big enough
to mess it up for us
cause a world of hurt
and i will still love you
all the same
i don't condone any of it

salt on my wounds
i can never go back
but i don't want you to have
to carry the weight of what
was never yours anymore
and i want you to know
that i am okay
no need to worry about me
i am finding my way
back home just fine
the healing finds me
all the same
and so i hope and
pray that your days
are long and sweet
that you rest well
and laugh with good friends
that you find joy and
know healing just as i did
and all i can say is that
you are lovely
and so beloved
and i wish nothing but
grace and freedom for you
for the rest of your days
thank you for the gift you were
thank you for the heartbreak you gave
it all makes sense
it all leads up to this moment
after it all, i find a love letter
in my heart for you too

-forgiveness

the messy in-between

i'm running out of ways
to tell you *i love you*
i could fill an entire book and
it still wouldn't feel like enough
i write you so many love letters
i almost forget about myself
but i wait for the words
and they slowly come

the messy in-between

and i know that you are afraid
i know that life has not
always been kind to you
come and stay for a little while
no need to bring anything
just come as you are
i know that there has not always
been enough space for you
but i am here now and
you can come home
whenever you're ready
take your time and
learn how to be loved again
i am sorry it has been so busy
i am sorry i wanted to be perfect
you don't have to be like that around me
can i get you anything while i'm up
a cup of tea or a soft place to land
have you eaten recently
are you tired from your journey
i hated you for so long
pretending i was something i'm not
i used to run, but i see you clearly now
you are not my enemy
you are not something to be afraid of
you are my fearful, childlike self
we move through our days together
i can tell that you are afraid still
we laugh and cry and dance
i tuck you into bed every night
i cannot help but love what i find

you are me, more honest and weak
the missing puzzle piece after all this time
the longer you stay
the more human i feel
i forgot a long time ago
i know it still hurts, it hurts me too
but i will not leave you again
i will stay this time and
you will not be alone like before
your trauma is not your fault
there's nothing you did to deserve it
your emotions are valid
and your fear is real
thank you for trying to protect us
i will keep us safe this time
and i know you are used to
feeling like you are not enough
but you are all that i need now
we can rest easy and heal slow
your story will be honored here
and i know that you are afraid still
i know that life has not
always been kind to you
come and stay for a little while
there is no need to bring anything
just come as you are
i know that there hasn't always
been enough space for you
but i am here now and
i cannot help but love when
you come back home to me

*inspired by aundi kolber

the messy in-between

they never told me
just how long the
healing would take
that the only way
past was through
no arriving on
this side of eternity
just pretty views

i am so tired of being broken
of life hurting like this
of looking like the monster
i said i would never become
how do i forgive myself
for all that i did not know yet
how do i dare to heal when
i don't even love myself

my past catches up to me
every single time
i've tried everything
the therapy
and the art
but the journey
costs me everything
and hurts too much

years have passed
but i still feel the abuse
pounding in my head
i run from anything
that reminds me of you
learn to mistake
broken and imperfect
for unworthy of love

i am on my knees
repenting again
crawling out of this desert
with my bare hands
i wander home in
dark storms and quiet waters
hold the beauty and depth
of another sunset

my feet follow the sun as it rises
dance with me underneath the stars
carry me as i write love letters
to a big, beautiful
and broken world
the journey is good, bad, ugly
and hard, but i am learning
to come home all the while

the messy in-between

everything has been leading up this moment
4 years sitting on my therapist's couch
3 years writing this book
i hurt and heal
break and become something new
learn to forgive myself
for being human
i fall back in love with life
and cotton candy skies
remember love can be soft and kind
even after them
and a couple of years later
i have survived the abuse and
become an empire overnight
i got tired of hating myself
for loving you and
blaming myself for things
that were never my fault
i needed my mind to be my own again
and so i took it back
and wrote poetry
and for all that i am
still figuring out
i am learning how to
be gentle with myself
i have lived a lot of life
had my heart broken a couple of times
done the hard work of
staying soft and gentle all the while
and at the end of the day
i think i have come a long way
and i am home now

-*homecoming*

special thank you:

cover by christina bagley and kelsey yin

reviews by natalie louie, sally kim, reilly carson, and kari nolasco

inspirations:

rupi kaur
morgan harper nichols
"try softer" by aundi kolber
"with a cap and gown and broken heart"
by jacob zelinski
"two" by sleeping at last
"beautiful things" by gungor
"queen songs / human" by judah & the lion
matthew 11:28-30 (the message)
mark 11:22-23 (niv) & 1 corinthians 13:4-8 (niv)

CPSIA information can be obtained
at www.ICGtesting.com
Printed in the USA
FSHW021252180521
81591FS